Tigerlily's Great Escape

Tanya Leighton

Dedicated to my niece Elysia. xxx

Tigerlily lived in a zoo, but she didn't fit in and her fur was blue too.

"Why oh why don't I look like my friends.
My fur is not orange, It's nothing like Glenn's."

Tigerlily

"I have an idea" Tigerlily said to the ape.

"I will leave this place, it will be the greatest escape."

The apes just laughed and swung on the trees,
Tigerlily thought, just you wait and see.

I am a blue Tiger and I don't fit in here, Just you wait till I disappear.

Tigerlily said to the tall giraffe

"I have something to tell you, but please don't laugh."

I am a blue Tiger and I don't fit in here,
Just you wait till I disappear.

Tigerlily walked away and went to see the elephant.

"Please don't laugh at me, I am feeling rather delicate."

"I have some news to share with you, I've made up my mind, I'm leaving the zoo!"

The elephant let out a very loud grumble.

She laughed so hard, it made the ground rumble.

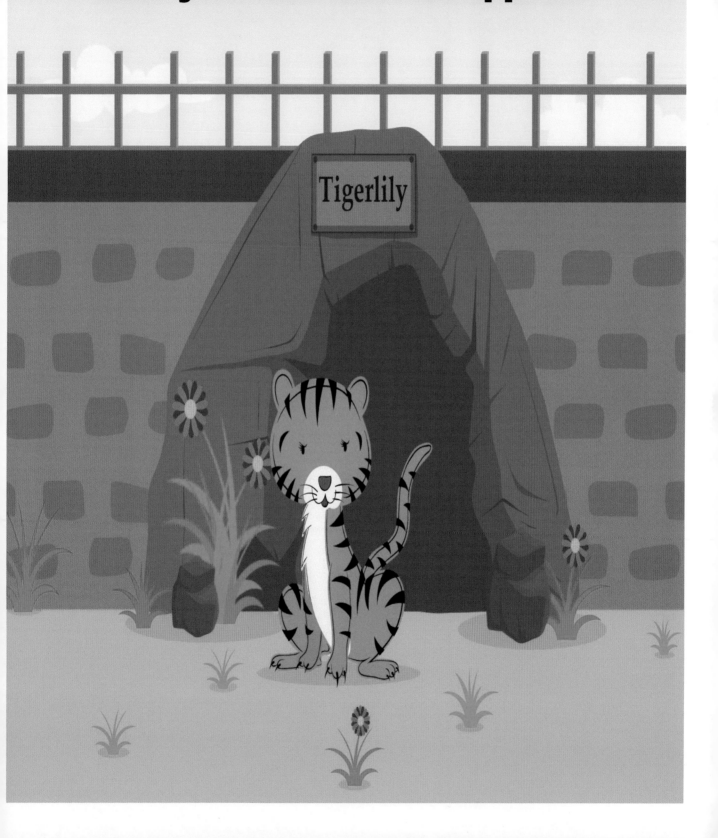

I am a blue Tiger and I don't fit in here,
Just you wait till I disappear.

Tigerlily went back to the den, to pack her bags, she was leaving at ten.

But the Tigers were all gathered there, looking very sad.

Tigerlily said

"has something happened? Is it really bad?"

"Of course it is bad, you're leaving" they said,

"Now we're all sad" said the Tiger named Fred.

The Tigers all smiled and hugged Tigerlily,

"We are so sorry, I'm afraid we've been silly."

"From now on you have nothing to fear, we want you to know that we are all here."

Don't listen to elephant, giraffe or ape and please, please, please don't try to escape.

Questions

How do you think Tigerlily felt when the ape, giraffe and elephant laughed at her plans?

What do you think the ape, giraffe and elephant should have said to Tigerlily instead of laughing?

Why did Tigerlily think her fur was blue?

How can we tell if someone might be sad?

How can we make them feel better?

What should you do if YOU feel sad?

What is anxiety?

How can we help our friends if we feel worried?

Can you think of a time that you felt worried?

<u>Help</u>

Depression and anxiety affects many children and adults.

There are things you can do to feel happy, less worried, scared or nervous.

Talk to an adult like a parent or a teacher.

You can also call Childline which is free and confidential on: 08001111

Signs and symptoms of childhood Depression

The child is no longer interested in activities that he/she once enjoyed.

There is a change in the child's appetite and/or sleep pattern.

The child has become withdrawn.

The child has become irritable and crying more than usual.

Signs and symptoms of childhood anxiety

The child may use lots of 'what if's'

The child may need excessive Reassurance.

The child may complain more than usual about physical problems.

The child is easily distressed.

The child may lie more than usual.

The child is a perfectionist.

Symptoms vary from child to child and these signs and symptoms are normal, healthy behaviours in many children.

If you have any concerns please see your GP.

Email: Mindfulness4children1@gmail.com

@Mindfulness4children1

Printed in Great Britain
by Amazon